Michael Phelps

Inspiring Story of the Olympic Legend

Satish Wanarse

INDEX

Preface

This novel tells the inspiring story of Michael Phelps, one of the greatest swimmers of all time. From his early years growing up in Baltimore, to his record-breaking performances at the Olympics, to his personal struggles and comeback, and to his legacy and future plans, this book takes readers on a journey through the life of a true champion.

Through the pages of this book, readers will learn about Phelps's unwavering dedication to his craft, his indomitable spirit, and his remarkable resilience. They will be inspired by his triumphs in the pool and moved by his honest portrayal of his personal struggles. Above all, they will come away with a deeper understanding of what it takes to succeed at the highest levels and how one person can make a lasting impact on the world.

The story of Michael Phelps is not just a story about swimming. It is a story about perseverance, determination, and the power of the human spirit. It is a story that will inspire readers of all ages and backgrounds to pursue their dreams, no matter how big or daunting they may seem.

I hope that this book will serve as a source of inspiration and motivation for readers everywhere. May it remind us that anything is possible if we have the courage to chase our dreams and the resilience to overcome obstacles along the way.

Chapter 1

The Early Years

Michael Phelps was born in Baltimore, Maryland, on June 30th, 1985. His parents, Debbie and Fred Phelps, were both teachers, and they raised Michael and his two older sisters, Whitney and Hilary, in a middle-class neighborhood.

From a young age, Michael was drawn to the water. His sisters were both swimmers, and he followed in their footsteps. When Michael was just seven years old, he started training at the Meadowbrook Aquatic Club, a local swimming club in Baltimore.

At Meadowbrook, Michael quickly distinguished himself as a talented swimmer. Despite his young age, it was clear that he had a natural affinity for the water. He was dedicated and focused, and he always pushed himself to be better.

Michael's parents recognized his potential and did everything they could to support his swimming. They drove him to and from the pool every day and never missed one of his swim meets.

As Michael continued to train and compete, he began to set himself apart from the other young swimmers. He broke his first national record at the age of 10 and continued to break records and win competitions as he got older.

One of the most significant events of Michael's early swimming career came when he was just 15 years old. At the 2000 Summer Olympics in Sydney, Australia, Michael became the youngest male swimmer to make the U.S. Olympic team in 68 years.

While Michael did not win a medal in Sydney, he gained invaluable experience and a taste of what it was like to compete at the highest level of swimming. He returned home to Baltimore even more determined to become the best swimmer he could be.

Despite his success in the pool, Michael faced challenges outside of it. As a child, he was diagnosed with Attention Deficit Hyperactivity Disorder (ADHD), which made it difficult for him to focus in school. Michael struggled with the condition for many years, but his parents and coaches worked with him to help him manage it.

Through swimming, Michael found an outlet for his energy and a way to channel his focus. He learned discipline and perseverance, and he began to see how hard work could lead to success.

As Michael grew older, he continued to excel in swimming. He broke world records, won Olympic medals, and became a household name. But it all started with a young boy who loved the water and was willing to work hard to achieve his dreams.

Michael Phelps's early years are a testament to the power of dedication and hard work. He may have had a natural talent for swimming, but it was his determination and focus that made him one of the greatest swimmers of all time. And it all began with a love for the water and a family who supported him every step of the way.

Chapter 2

The First Olympics

Michael Phelps had been swimming competitively since he was just seven years old. He had broken records and won numerous competitions, but the ultimate goal for any swimmer is to compete in the Olympics.

Phelps qualified for his first Olympics when he was just 15 years old. The 2000 Sydney Olympics were a turning point for him. He didn't win any medals, but he gained valuable experience and set his sights on the next Olympics.

Phelps was the youngest male swimmer to make the U.S. Olympic team in 68 years, and he was eager to prove himself on the world stage. He competed in the 200-meter butterfly, the 200-meter individual medley, and the 400-meter individual medley.

In his first event, the 200-meter butterfly, Phelps finished fifth in the final. He was disappointed, but he knew that he had given it his all. In the 200-meter individual medley, Phelps finished sixth in the final. And in the 400-meter individual medley, Phelps finished fifth in the final.

While Phelps didn't win any medals in Sydney, he gained invaluable experience and set his sights on the next Olympics. He was determined to improve and come back stronger than ever.

Phelps's performance in Sydney showed that he was a force to be reckoned with in the world of swimming. He may not have won any medals, but he had made a name for himself on the international stage.

After the Olympics, Phelps returned home to Baltimore and resumed his training. He continued to work hard and set his sights on the 2004 Olympics in Athens, Greece.

Phelps knew that he had to improve if he wanted to be successful at the Olympics. He worked on his technique, his endurance, and his mental toughness. He pushed himself harder than ever before and dedicated himself to his training.

In the four years between the Sydney Olympics and the Athens Olympics, Phelps became one of the most dominant swimmers in the world. He broke multiple world records and won countless competitions.

Phelps's success was not without its challenges, however. He faced criticism from some who felt that he was too focused on winning and not enjoying the sport of swimming. Phelps, however, remained dedicated to his goals and continued to work hard.

As the 2004 Olympics approached, Phelps was ready. He had trained for years and was determined to bring home gold medals. His performance in Athens would cement his place in history as one of the greatest swimmers of all time.

The 2000 Sydney Olympics may not have resulted in any medals for Michael Phelps, but they were a pivotal moment in his career. They showed him what it takes to compete at the highest level and set him on a path to greatness. Phelps's journey to the Olympics was just beginning, and the world was about to witness one of the most dominant athletes in history.

Chapter 3

Breaking Records

Michael Phelps had already made his mark on the swimming world, but he was just getting started. He had a fire inside him that drove him to be the best. And he wasn't going to let anyone or anything stand in his way.

As he continued to train and compete, Phelps started to break records. His incredible speed and technique were unmatched, and he quickly became known as one of the greatest swimmers of all time. He was breaking world records left and right, and he didn't show any signs of slowing down.

The first world record that Phelps broke was in the 200m butterfly. He set the record at the 2001 World Championships in Fukuoka, Japan, with a time of

1:53.93. This was a huge accomplishment for Phelps, and it was just the beginning.

Over the next few years, Phelps would continue to break records in the 200m butterfly, as well as other events. In 2003, at the World Championships in Barcelona, Spain, Phelps broke the world record in the 400m individual medley. He finished with a time of 4:09.09, beating the previous record by over a second.

Phelps was on fire, and he continued to set new records at the 2004 Athens Olympics. He won six gold medals and two bronze medals, breaking two world records in the process. His performance was nothing short of incredible, and he had cemented his status as a legend in the world of swimming.

But Phelps wasn't content with just breaking records. He wanted to push himself even further, to see just how fast he could go. He was always looking for ways to improve his technique and his training, and he was never satisfied with anything less than his best.

In 2007, at the World Championships in Melbourne, Australia, Phelps broke the world record in the 200m freestyle. He finished with a time of 1:43.86, beating the previous record by over half a second. This was a huge accomplishment, and it showed that Phelps was still at the top of his game.

But Phelps wasn't done yet. In 2008, at the Beijing Olympics, he set his sights on breaking even more records. And he did just that. He won eight gold medals, breaking seven world records in the process. His performance was nothing short of legendary, and he had achieved what many thought was impossible.

Phelps had proven that he was the greatest swimmer of all time. He had broken more records than anyone else, and he had done it with style and grace. But he wasn't done yet. He had more goals to achieve, more records to break, and more races to win.

Phelps's incredible journey was far from over. But as he looked back on everything he had accomplished, he knew that he had already made history. He had broken records, won championships, and become an inspiration to millions around the world. And he had done it all with a smile on his face, a fire in his heart, and a determination that would never waver.

Chapter 4

The 2004 Olympics

The Olympics are the ultimate stage for any athlete, and Michael Phelps was no exception. After a disappointing showing in the 2000 Sydney Olympics, Phelps was determined to make his mark in the 2004 Athens Olympics.

Phelps had spent the past four years training relentlessly, perfecting his strokes and building his endurance. He had his sights set on the ultimate goal: to win as many gold medals as possible.

When Phelps arrived in Athens, he was confident and ready. He had already made a name for himself in the swimming world, but he knew that the Olympics were where he could truly cement his legacy.

Phelps wasted no time getting to work. In his first event, the 400m individual medley, he set a new world record and won the gold medal. It was the first of many victories for Phelps in the 2004 Olympics.

Over the course of the next few days, Phelps continued to dominate in the pool. He won gold medals in the 100m and 200m butterfly, the 200m and 400m individual medleys, and the 4x200m freestyle relay.

But Phelps wasn't done yet. He had his sights set on a new goal: to break the record for the most gold medals won in a single Olympics. The record was currently held by Mark Spitz, who had won seven gold medals in the 1972 Olympics.

Phelps had a chance to tie the record in the 100m freestyle relay. The pressure was on, but Phelps was ready. He swam the second leg of the relay and helped his team secure the gold medal.

Phelps had now won seven gold medals, tying Spitz's record. But he wasn't satisfied. He still had one more event to go: the 4x100m medley relay.

The medley relay was the final event of the Olympics, and it was the last chance for Phelps to break the record. He swam the butterfly leg of the relay, and he did not disappoint. He swam the fastest butterfly leg in history, helping his team win the gold medal and giving him his eighth gold medal of the Olympics.

Phelps had done it. He had broken the record for the most gold medals won in a single Olympics. He had won eight gold medals and set four world records in the process. He was now a legend in the world of swimming.

The 2004 Olympics were a turning point for Phelps. He had proven that he was not just a talented swimmer, but a dominant force in the sport. He had shown the world what was possible when you set your sights on a goal and work tirelessly to achieve it.

Phelps's performance in the 2004 Olympics was historic, and it set the stage for even greater accomplishments in the future. He had become a hero to people around the world, and his legacy was just beginning to take shape.

Chapter 5

Personal Struggles

Michael Phelps's success in the pool was unparalleled, but his personal life was a different story. Despite his numerous accolades and achievements, he struggled with depression, anxiety, and substance abuse. This chapter will explore Phelps's personal struggles, how he hit rock bottom, and how he emerged from this dark period stronger and more determined than ever.

It's hard to imagine that someone as successful as Michael Phelps could be struggling with mental health issues. But fame and fortune don't protect you from the challenges of life. Phelps was no exception. His struggles with depression and anxiety were something that he kept hidden from the public eye for years. It wasn't until he hit rock bottom that he realized he needed help.

Phelps has been very open about his struggles with mental health, including his battle with depression. In an interview with CNN, he spoke about how he would go days without leaving his room or talking to anyone. "I didn't want to be in the sport anymore," he said. "I didn't want to be alive."

Phelps's struggles with substance abuse were also well-documented. He was arrested for driving under the influence in 2004 and 2014. The second arrest was a wake-up call for Phelps. He realized that he needed to seek help and get his life back on track.

In 2015, Phelps entered a rehabilitation program. He spent six weeks in treatment, working with a therapist to address his mental health issues and learn coping skills. Phelps also began to attend Alcoholics Anonymous meetings and work with a sponsor. He took his recovery seriously and worked hard to stay sober.

During this time, Phelps also began to work on himself outside of the pool. He got engaged to his long-time girlfriend, Nicole Johnson, and the couple welcomed their first child, Boomer, in 2016. Phelps credits his family with helping him to stay on track and giving him a new perspective on life.

Phelps's journey to recovery wasn't easy, but it was worth it. He emerged from his struggles stronger and more determined than ever. In an interview with Today, Phelps spoke about how he now views his struggles as a gift. "I'm still going to have struggles in my life, but I now know how to deal with them," he said. "I have the tools and resources to help me get through those tough times."

Phelps's story is a reminder that even the most successful people can struggle with mental health issues. It's okay to seek help and take time to work on yourself. Phelps's journey to recovery shows that with hard work and dedication, it is possible to overcome even the toughest of challenges.

Phelps's journey to recovery also shows the importance of having a support system. He credits his family, friends, and therapist with helping him to stay on track. If you or someone you know is struggling with mental health issues or substance abuse, it's important to reach out for help. There are resources available, and you don't have to go through it alone.

In conclusion, Phelps's personal struggles were a difficult chapter in his life, but they also served as a turning point. He hit rock bottom and realized that he needed help. He took the necessary steps to seek treatment and work on himself. Phelps emerged from this dark period stronger and more determined than ever. His story is a reminder that it's okay to ask for help and take time to work on yourself.

Chapter 6

The 2008 Olympics

The 2008 Beijing Olympics were the culmination of Michael Phelps's career. He had already won a record eight medals in Athens in 2004, but the 2008 games presented an opportunity for him to break even more records and cement his legacy as the greatest swimmer of all time.

Phelps arrived in Beijing with the weight of the world on his shoulders. The media had hyped up his quest for eight gold medals, and fans were eagerly awaiting his performances. But Phelps remained focused on his goals and didn't let the pressure get to him.

The first event on Phelps's schedule was the 400-meter individual medley. It was a tough race, but Phelps managed to pull ahead in the final stretch and win gold. It was the start of an incredible run that would make Olympic history.

Over the next few days, Phelps continued to dominate in the pool. He won gold medals in the 4x100-meter freestyle relay, the 200-meter freestyle, the 200-meter butterfly, and the 4x200-meter freestyle relay. He also set world records in the 200-meter freestyle and the 200-meter butterfly.

Phelps's performance in the 200-meter butterfly was particularly impressive. He was up against Serbia's Milorad Čavić, who had been talking trash in the media leading up to the event. Čavić took an early lead and was ahead of Phelps coming into the final stretch. But Phelps managed to out-touch him at the wall, winning by just one-hundredth of a second. It was a thrilling race and showed Phelps's determination and ability to come from behind.

Next up was the 200-meter individual medley, another tough event. Phelps was up against his biggest rival, Ryan Lochte. But Phelps once again proved to be the better swimmer, winning gold and setting a new world record.

With six gold medals under his belt, Phelps was just two away from breaking his own record from Athens. The 100-meter butterfly was up next, and it was a nail-biting race. Phelps and Čavić were once again neck and neck, but this time it was Čavić who had the lead coming into the final stretch. But Phelps managed to make up ground and out-touch him at the wall, winning by just one-hundredth of a second. It was another incredible race and showed Phelps's ability to perform under pressure.

Phelps's seventh gold medal came in the 4x100-meter medley relay. It was the last race of the games, and Phelps swam the butterfly leg. He once again proved to be the key to the American team's victory, helping them set a new world record.

Phelps's eight gold medals in Beijing broke his own record and made him the most successful Olympian of all time. He had achieved what many thought was impossible, and the world was in awe of his incredible performances.

But for Phelps, the journey was far from over. He knew that he still had more to accomplish and more records to break. The 2012 London Olympics were just four years away, and Phelps was already looking ahead to the next challenge.

Chapter 7

Retirement a New Chapter Begins

After four Olympic Games, 28 medals (23 of them gold), and countless broken records, Michael Phelps announced his retirement from competitive swimming. It was the end of an era for the sport, and the beginning of a new chapter in Phelps's life.

Retirement didn't come easy for Phelps, who had dedicated his entire life to swimming. It was his passion, his identity, and his ticket to worldwide fame. But Phelps knew it was time to move on and start a new phase in his life.

"I accomplished everything I wanted to in the sport," Phelps said in a press conference announcing his retirement. "I'm ready for the next chapter."

The next chapter, however, wasn't immediately clear. Phelps had spent most of his life training and competing, leaving little room for anything else. But he was determined to find new goals and passions, outside of the pool.

"I know it's going to be a challenge," Phelps said. "But I'm excited to see what's next."

Retirement gave Phelps the chance to focus on his family. He had gotten married to his long-time girlfriend, Nicole Johnson, in a secret ceremony a few months before retiring. The couple had a son, Boomer, and later two more children, Beckett and Maverick. Phelps enjoyed being a present father and spending more time with his family.

"I didn't realize how much I was missing out on," Phelps said about fatherhood. "Being able to be there for every moment is something I cherish."

Phelps also dedicated his time to his foundation, the Michael Phelps Foundation, which aims to promote water safety and swimming. He believed that swimming had given him so much in life, and he wanted to give back to the sport that had shaped him into the person he was today.

"It's not just about teaching kids how to swim," Phelps said. "It's about giving them the tools to succeed in life, to be confident and determined."

Phelps also took on new challenges outside of the pool. He became a commentator for NBC during the Rio 2016 Olympics, providing insights and analysis on swimming events. He also made appearances in TV shows, commercials, and events, becoming a sought-after celebrity.

But Phelps's post-swimming life wasn't without struggles. Retirement brought a new set of challenges, including finding a new purpose and dealing with mental health issues.

Phelps had struggled with depression and anxiety for most of his life, and retirement amplified those issues. Without the structure and discipline of swimming, Phelps found himself struggling with his mental health.

"It's not something that just goes away," Phelps said about depression. "It's something I have to manage every day."

Phelps became an advocate for mental health awareness, opening up about his own struggles and encouraging others to seek help.

"I want people to know that it's okay to not be okay," Phelps said. "There's no shame in asking for help."

Retirement also gave Phelps the opportunity to reflect on his legacy. He had achieved more than any other swimmer in history, but he also faced scrutiny and criticism for his past mistakes, including a DUI arrest in 2014.

"I'm not perfect," Phelps said. "I've made mistakes, and I've learned from them."

Phelps hoped that his legacy would be more than just his medals and records, but also his impact on the sport and his advocacy for causes he cared about.

"I want to be remembered as someone who made a difference," Phelps said.

Phelps's retirement marked the end of an era in swimming, but it also marked the beginning of a new chapter in his life. Retirement wasn't easy, but Phelps faced it with the same determination and discipline that had made him a champion in the

pool

Chapter 8

Comeback of Legend

Michael Phelps had retired from swimming after the 2012 London Olympics, but he couldn't stay away for long. In 2014, Phelps announced that he was making a comeback and aiming for the 2016 Rio Olympics. Fans around the world were excited to see what the legendary swimmer had in store.

However, Phelps's comeback wasn't smooth sailing. He had to overcome personal struggles and physical setbacks to get back to his winning ways.

Phelps had struggled with depression, anxiety, and substance abuse after the 2012 Olympics. He had hit rock bottom and even contemplated suicide. But with the help of therapy and support from his family and friends, he was able to overcome his demons and come out stronger.

Once Phelps had his personal life back on track, he turned his attention to his physical conditioning. He knew that he needed to be in the best shape of his life to compete at the highest level again.

Phelps worked with his longtime coach, Bob Bowman, to come up with a training plan that would get him back to his winning ways. He also worked with a nutritionist to make sure he was fueling his body with the right foods.

The road back to the top was not easy. Phelps faced stiff competition from up-and-coming swimmers who were eager to dethrone the king. He also had to deal with injuries, including a torn labrum in his shoulder.

But Phelps didn't let these setbacks get him down. He knew that he had the talent and the drive to succeed. He pushed himself to the limit in training, putting in countless hours in the pool and the weight room.

As the 2016 Rio Olympics approached, Phelps was back in peak form. He had qualified for multiple events and was poised to add to his already impressive medal count.

The world watched in awe as Phelps dominated in the pool once again. He won five gold medals and a silver medal, bringing his total medal count to 28. He had become the most decorated Olympian of all time.

Phelps's comeback was a testament to his resilience and determination. He had faced some of the toughest challenges of his life, but he never gave up. He proved that anything is possible with hard work, dedication, and a never-give-up attitude.

Fans around the world were inspired by Phelps's comeback story. He had shown that no matter how far you fall, you can always get back up again. Phelps's legacy as one of the greatest athletes of all time was secure, but his comeback added another chapter to his incredible story.

Phelps retired from swimming again after the 2016 Olympics, but his comeback will always be remembered as one of the greatest in sports history. It showed that even the greatest athletes face adversity, but with perseverance and determination, they can overcome anything.

Chapter 9

Legacy

Michael Phelps is more than just a swimming legend. He's a role model, an inspiration, and a true champion in every sense of the word. His legacy goes far beyond his 28 Olympic medals, and his impact on the sport of swimming and the world at large cannot be overstated.

Phelps's journey to becoming the most decorated Olympian of all time wasn't easy. He faced personal struggles, setbacks, and challenges throughout his career. But through it all, he never gave up. He kept pushing himself to be better, to swim faster, and to reach new heights.

Phelps's legacy is a testament to the power of hard work, dedication, and perseverance. He proved that with the right mindset, anything is possible.

And he inspired a generation of swimmers to follow in his footsteps and chase their dreams.

Phelps's impact on the sport of swimming is immeasurable. He raised the bar for what was possible, not just in terms of his medal count, but in terms of the way he approached the sport. His technique, his focus, and his drive to constantly improve set a new standard for swimmers around the world.

Phelps also helped to popularize swimming and bring it into the mainstream. He made the sport exciting and accessible to people who may have never considered it before. And he inspired countless kids and adults to get into the pool and start swimming themselves.

But Phelps's impact goes beyond just the sport of swimming. He has been an outspoken advocate for mental health, using his platform to raise awareness and encourage others to seek help when they need it. He has also been a leader in promoting water safety and drowning prevention, using his own personal experiences to help others stay safe in and around the water.

Phelps's authenticity and honesty about his struggles have made him a relatable figure to fans around the world. He's not just a superhuman athlete; he's a real person who has faced real challenges. And that's what makes his legacy so powerful.

Phelps's impact on the world will continue long after his retirement from competitive swimming. He has already made a difference in the lives of countless people, and his influence will be felt for generations to come. He has shown us all what it means to be a champion, both in and out of the pool.

As we look back on Michael Phelps's incredible career, we can't help but be inspired. He showed us that with hard work, dedication, and a little bit of perseverance, we can achieve anything we set our minds to. And he proved that even the greatest champions face struggles and setbacks, but it's how we respond to those challenges that truly defines us.

Michael Phelps will always be remembered as one of the greatest athletes of all time, but his legacy is so much more than just his medal count. He's an inspiration to us all, a symbol of what we can achieve when we believe in ourselves and refuse to give up. He's a true champion in every sense of the word, and his impact on the world will never be forgotten.

Chapter 10

The Future

Michael Phelps's swimming career is behind him, but he is far from done making an impact on the world. As he looks to the future, Phelps is excited about the opportunities that lie ahead. He is focused on his family, his foundation, and his business ventures. Phelps has left his mark on the world of swimming, and his legacy will continue to inspire for generations to come.

Phelps has always been a family man, and his retirement from swimming has given him more time to spend with his loved ones. He is happily married to his wife, Nicole, and they have three children together. Phelps has said that fatherhood has given him a new sense of purpose and fulfillment.

In addition to spending time with his family, Phelps is also committed to his foundation, the Michael Phelps Foundation. The foundation's mission is to promote water safety and encourage children to lead healthy, active lifestyles. Phelps has said that he wants to use his platform to make a positive impact on the world, and his foundation is a major part of that.

Phelps is also involved in several business ventures. He has partnered with companies like Under Armour, Omega, and Colgate to promote their products. Phelps has also invested in tech startups and other businesses. He has said that he wants to use his success to help others succeed, too.

Despite his retirement from swimming, Phelps is still connected to the sport. He is a commentator for NBC Sports during major swimming events, and he is often called upon to offer his insights and expertise. Phelps is also a coach and mentor to young swimmers, and he is passionate about helping the next generation of athletes reach their full potential.

Phelps's legacy as a swimmer is unparalleled. He is the most successful Olympian of all time, with 28 medals to his name. But Phelps's impact goes beyond his medal count. He inspired a generation of swimmers and showed that anything is possible with hard work and dedication. Phelps's authenticity and honesty about his struggles made him relatable to fans around the world.

Phelps has been open about his battles with depression, anxiety, and substance abuse. He has said that seeking help was the best decision he ever made, and he wants others to know that they are not alone. Phelps's honesty about his struggles has helped to reduce the stigma around mental health, and he has become a powerful advocate for those who are struggling.

Phelps's legacy as a swimmer and as a human being is secure. He has achieved more than most people could ever dream of, but he remains humble and grounded. Phelps has said that he wants to be remembered not just as a swimmer, but as someone who made a positive impact on the world.

As he looks to the future, Phelps is excited about the opportunities that lie ahead. He knows that his swimming career is behind him, but he is ready for the next chapter of his life. Phelps's dedication to his family, his foundation, and his business ventures shows that he is committed to making a difference in the world. And as he continues to inspire others with his authenticity and his determination, Phelps's legacy will continue to shine bright for years to come.

Printed in Great Britain
by Amazon

56847604R00030

Mike Jenkins's first two books of poems and stories in Merthyr dialect were published by 'Planet'. Since then, Carreg Gwalch have published 'Barkin!' which was long-listed for Wales Book of the Year and also 'Sofa Surfin'. He has published two books of dialect poetry with the leftwing co-operative 'Culture Matters', for whom he is editing an anthology of dialect poetry from Cymru, entitled 'Yer Ower Voices!', with poems in English and Welsh.

In *Barkin!* Mike Jenkins captures both the craziness and tragedy of his home town. These are poems and stories, using Merthyr's vibrant vernacular, about people who try to defy the oppression of a system which has made it one of the poorest places in the land.
Poems and stories, written in the Merthyr dialect, was shortlisted for Wales Book of the Year in 2014.

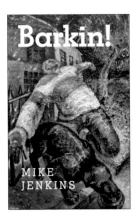

£7.50

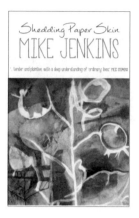

The title poem marks Mike Jenkins' transition from the teaching profession to a free-ranging life thereafter. In this new collection of his work, there's a wide variety of subject-matter and approach.

£7.50

A second collection of poems by Mike Jenkins, comprising humorous and poignant portraits of colourful characters from the poet's native Merthyr Tydfil, with some poems focusing on the 1966 Aberfan disaster and on people facing benefit cuts.

£7.50

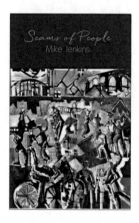

This collection by Mike Jenkins moves from opening poems about Wales and the possibilities of independence, to an ending of three poems based in Corfu.

£7.50